MAGIC MONSTERS
Look for Shapes

by Jane Belk Moncure
illustrated by Diana Magnuson

THE
CHILD'S
WORLD

ELGIN, ILLINOIS 60120

Distributed by Childrens Press, 1224 West Van Buren Street, Chicago, Illinois 60607.

Library of Congress Cataloging in Publication Data

Moncure, Jane Belk.
  Magic monsters look for shapes.

  (Magic monsters series)
  SUMMARY: The magic monsters introduce the basic shapes and find representative examples.
  [1. Size and shape—Fiction. 2. Monsters—Fiction]
I. Magnuson, Diana. II. Title. III. Series.
PZ7.M739Maj   [E]   78-21529
ISBN 0-89565-057-6

MAGIC MONSTERS
Look for Shapes

The magic monster apes
looked for shapes.

5

First they looked for

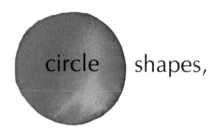

circle shapes,

shapes exactly round.

Here is what they found.

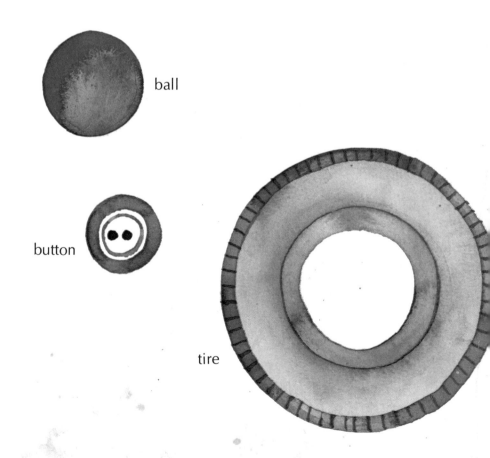

ball

button

tire

Count the circle shapes
the apes found.

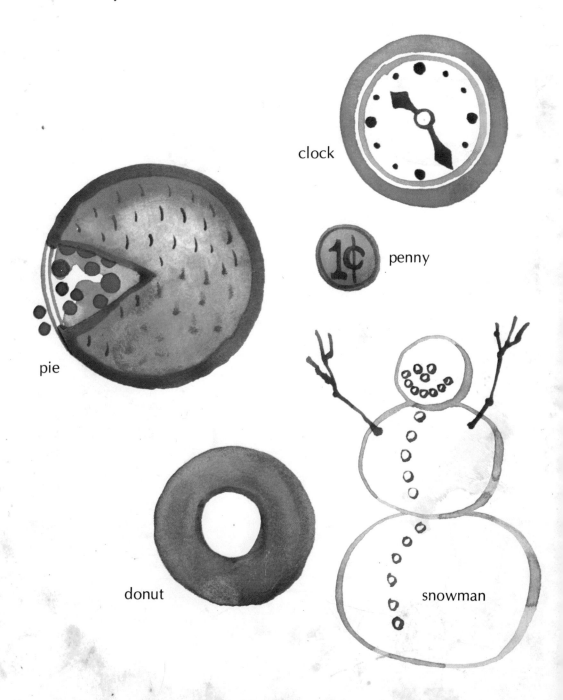

clock

pie

penny

donut

snowman

"These are little circle shapes,"
said the apes.
"We want to find
monster circle shapes."

So they went to the fair
and found monster circle
shapes there.

Then the apes looked for

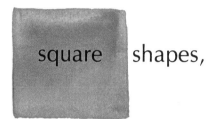 square shapes,

shapes with four sides
exactly the same.

Here is what they found.

book

zoo cage

Count the square shapes
the apes found.

checkerboard

tiles

window pane

"These are little square shapes,"
said the apes.
"We want to find
monster square shapes."

15

So they went to town and found
blocks in squares
for miles and miles,
monster squares all around.

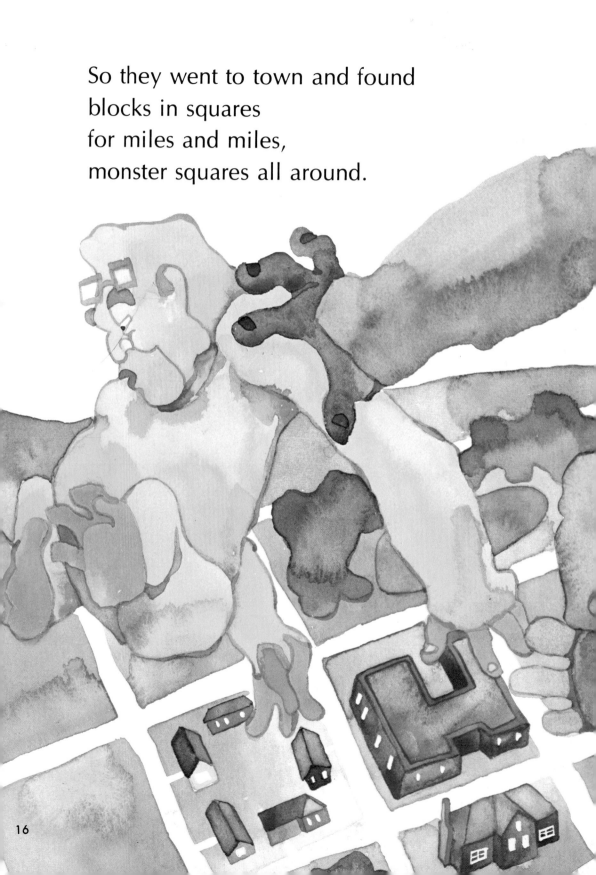

Then the apes looked for

rectangle shapes,

shapes with two short sides
exactly the same
and two long sides
exactly the same.

window

envelope

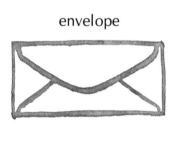

toy train

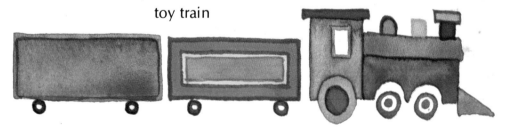

Count the rectangle shapes
the apes found.

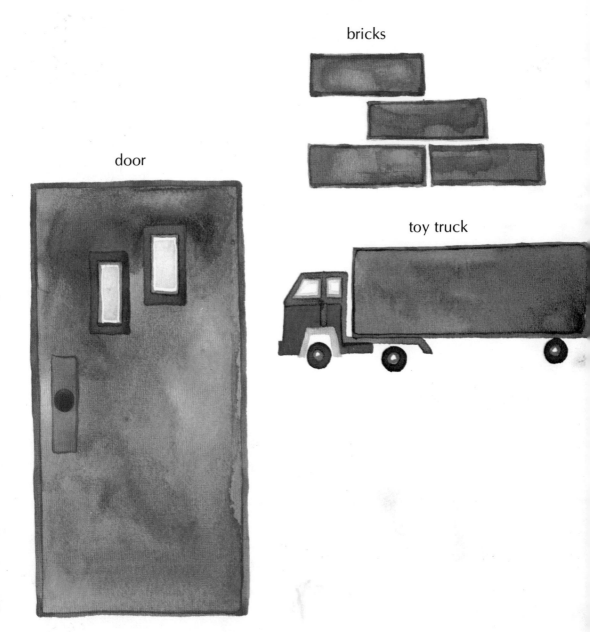

bricks

door

toy truck

"These are little rectangle shapes,"
said the apes.
"We want to find
monster rectangle shapes."

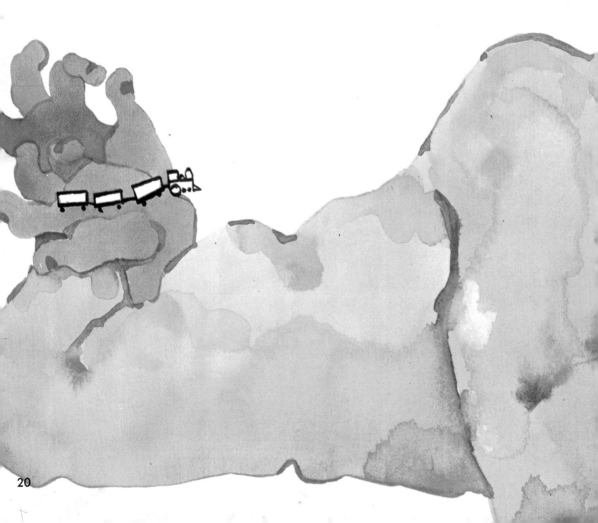

So they went to the city and found
monster rectangle shapes all around.

Then the apes looked for

triangle shapes,

shapes with three sides.

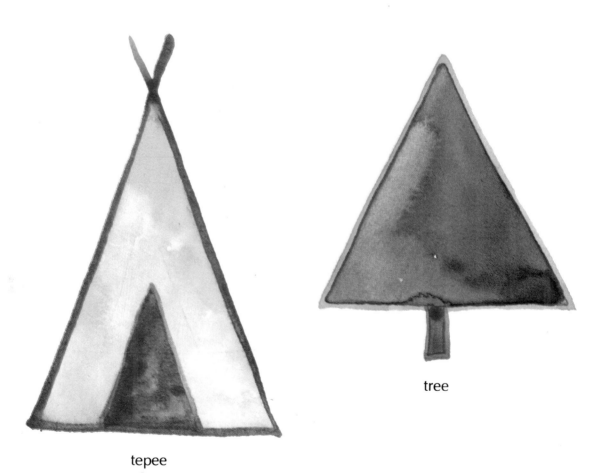

tepee

tree

Count the triangle shapes
the apes found.

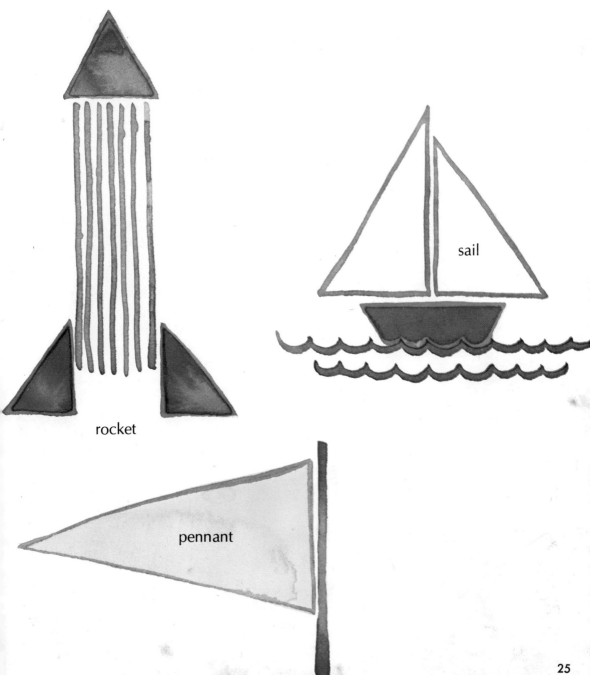

rocket

sail

pennant

"These are little triangle shapes,"
said the apes.
"We want to find
monster triangle shapes."

So they went to the mountains and found
monster triangle shapes all around.

Now, look at these things
the apes found.
Which are circles?
Which are squares?
Which are rectangles?
Which are triangles?

Can you find more shapes
for the magic monster apes?
Look all around.
Find little shapes
and monster shapes.